Peaches Can Do It!

By: Daphanny C.Baker

J MERRILL

For permission requests, please contact the Permissions Coordinator at:

J Merrill Publishing, Inc.
434 Hillpine Drive, Suite 100
Columbus, OH 43207
www.JMerrill.pub

Library of Congress Control Number: 2025915530
Paperback ISBN-13: 978-1-961475-47-2
eBook ISBN-13: 978-1-961475-48-9

Book Title: Peaches Can Do It!
Author: Daphanny C. Baker

Whether we use Biological, Adopted, Foster or Step...

It wasn't the word before Mom and Dad that made you my parents.. but rather the love, commitment and dedication that you gave a little girl that needed a rescue team! My Hero and Heroine, you both can rest easy knowing that you fulfilled your God-designed mission. The Missionaries of all Missionaries... I am forever Affected and Effected by your unselfish desire to put my Mom's heart at ease when the Lord left me here on earth.

Thank you for the gift of Hope! For it was because of you two that I was able to accomplish all that I have!

Here's to you BOTH! ❤️

FOREWORD

Every life is a story, and some stories are meant to be shared with the world. Lady Daphanny C. Baker's journey is one of resilience, faith, and inspiration—woven together with lessons that young hearts can carry for a lifetime. In these pages, children will discover more than just the events of her life; they will find a guiding light, a message of perseverance, and the warmth of a woman who has embraced life with purpose and love.

This book is not just a reflection of the past but a gift for the future. Lady Daphanny's story reminds us that every child has the power to overcome challenges, dream big, and walk boldly in their own unique path. As you turn each page, may you be encouraged to embrace your own journey with courage and joy.

With admiration and blessings,

— BISHOP MELVIN T BAKER, YOUR HUSBAND FOREVER

INTRODUCTION

Life can be challenging. We cannot dictate how our future will unfold.

Daphanny C. Baker's life was both unique and fascinating. At almost three years old, her world changed completely when her birth mother passed away. What would she do now? The Lord had already decided what would happen to her.

God's hand was on this little girl, who was taken in by family members. From that moment on, her future was set in motion.

Before she was even thought of, Daphanny—also known as **Peaches**—was destined for greatness. Both God and everyone she encountered knew it. She was capable of handling any situation that came her way. She was strong, persistent, and determined that nothing would derail her from her **God-given** assignment.

Her adoptive mother was so impressed by her resilience that she would always declare:

"Peaches can do it!"

She believed Peaches could overcome any challenge, no matter how big or difficult. That confidence became the inspiration for this book's title.

Because of the encouragement she received and her unwavering determination...

She **survived** it.

She **conquered** it.

She **got through** it.

And yes, she **mastered** it!

There once was a girl named Peaches...

Life was promising and full of possibilities.

Until one day, when her mommy got very sick—and then, she was gone.

Peaches was very, very sad.

She didn't know what to do.

She was all alone.

She went from house to house...

15

Knocking on doors.

"Will you take me?"

But she was turned away.

She tried again.

"Will you take me in?"

The answer was no.

No one wanted this little girl.

Until one day, a priest named Clifford and his wife, Doll-Face, found Peaches had nowhere to go.

They welcomed her into their home with open arms.

Peaches was overjoyed!

The couple loved her as if she were their own.

They taught her many things and raised her in the church.

Peaches sang in the choir!

People loved to hear her angelic voice.

She received a standing ovation every time.

Life had truly turned around for Peaches.

God had placed her with a wonderful set of bonus
parents.

Every night, Clifford and Doll-Face took turns tucking
Peaches in.

They made sure she felt loved and safe.

She had birthday parties every year.

She was always reminded how special she was.

But then... tragedy struck again.

At just nine years old, Peaches lost Clifford.

She was devastated.

"Why do I have to go through this again?" she wondered.

31

Now it was just Peaches and Doll-Face.

Though she grieved, Peaches was grateful to still have
Doll-Face by her side.

33

She continued to grow into a strong, young woman, thanks to the godly foundation that Doll-Face provided.

One day, Peaches met someone special.

She got married.

She was very, very happy!

FIVE GUYS

Erica   Yonna   Rey   Ti   LJ

Then something wonderful happened!

She had one... two... three... four... FIVE children!

Erica, Eryonna, Erskine, Diamond, and Javier

TOOT

Later, she even had a grand-girl—her name is Toot!

Peaches never stopped growing.

She was called to preach God's word!

The lessons from Clifford and Doll-Face had shaped her life.

They raised her to be a woman of tenacity and strength.

43

She was overjoyed!

Though she had lost in the beginning, she was winning in the end.

Her life proved that God had already mapped out her journey.

Her story is proof that...

Whether the sun is shining...

47

Whether it's raining...

Or whether there's an all-out storm...

51

If God has His hand on you—you will make it through!

Start...

The way you start... does not determine how you finish.

55

The enemy may think he's won.

He may believe he has knocked you down

happy

But that's when God steps in—

And you will WIN.

59

Peaches won in so many areas of her life.

She is now the wife of a pastor.

61

She has earned a Master of Business Administration (MBA) and a Master of Divinity.

365 Days of Transparency

Lady Daphanny's Altar

The Messenger

Peaches can do it!

LOADING♡♡♡

And if you're reading this...

She is now a four-time author!

Peaches Can Do It!

BELIEVE IN YOURSELF

You can if you say you can.

Peaches Can Do It!

Would Peaches have accomplished all of this without
these four words?

67

Affirming words go a long way—whether someone is encouraging you or you are encouraging yourself.

Just remember...

You can do it too!

With God on your side and a heart full of determination...

Stay in the race!

My Photo Album

My Birth Mom

Her | Me

My Birth Mom and I

Birth Mom, Myself and Adopted Mom

Adopted Parents

My Kindergarten Graduation

Adopted Mom and I

www.ingramcontent.com/pod-product-compliance
Lightning Source LLC
Chambersburg PA
CBHW041123120626
46547CB00019B/2825